How to Pet a Cat

How to Pet a Cat

Angela Staehling

CHRONICLE BOOKS

SAN FRANCISCO

Library of Congress Cataloging-in-Publication Data

Names: Staehling, Angela, author.
Title: How to pet a cat / Angela Staehling.
Description: San Francisco, CA : Chronicle Books, [2022] | Includes
    bibliographical references.
Identifiers: LCCN 2021031146 | 9781797211121 (hardcover)
Subjects: LCSH: Cats--Behavior. | Cats.
Classification: LCC SF446.5 .S73 2022 | DDC 636.8/083--dc23
LC record available at https://lccn.gov/2021031146

Manufactured in China.

Design by Kim Di Santo and Evelyn Furuta.

10 9 8 7 6 5 4 3 2 1

CHRONICLE BOOKS
680 SECOND STREET
SAN FRANCISCO, CA 94107
WWW.CHRONICLEBOOKS.COM

CONTENTS

Introduction

Understanding Your Cat

Petting Methods That Your Cat (*Usually*) Prefers

Petting Methods That Annoy Your Cat

Resources

Some Special Cats

To my cats, Rocco and Theo. They taught me everything there is to know about petting cats—namely that there's always room for improvement. I thank my kids, Cole, Mia, and Ella, for inspiring me to write this book.

While on vacation, missing our cats led to discussing all the different ways we pet our fur babes. The good, the bad, and the ugly—this book captures it all and will hopefully help you score points with your own feline friend.

Introduction

Have you ever noticed that cat owners get a little embarrassed to admit they're cat people? Whenever they confess they own a cat, it's as if they've done something shameful, like show up late to a party without even bothering to bring a gift. Cat people are a true breed unto themselves, and they're often made to feel apologetic for owning such furry lightweights compared to their canine counterparts. But cat people aren't bothered by all the hype and popularity of dogs, and it certainly won't stop them from adopting a cat. They see through the smoke and mirrors and know that cats are supreme beings.

Cats teach people a lot about the ways of the world, such as there being value in not breathing heavily in someone's face and being the slobbery center of attention. Cats are masters at the art of relaxation, and demonstrate how to strike at a moment's notice without alerting the opponent (this may come in handy when reaching for the last Oreo). They are our mini mentors. They reveal to us so much about the universe and how to live a more chill life.

One way to give thanks to our feline friends is to learn how to properly pet them. This book will guide you through the steps of feeling confident around your cat. The last thing you want is for your fluffball to feel that you are unworthy. Cats already give you the benefit of the doubt and consider you their equal, and having to take time out of their day to regard you as anything lesser than is very annoying.

UNDERSTANDING YOUR CAT

Personality Types

Our little fluff balls come in as many shapes, sizes, and personalities as there are stars in the night sky. While it might be easy to think that we "picked" our cat based on what we wanted—a cat who cuddles, a cat who plays, a cat who sleeps all day—it was the universe who sent our cat to us. After all, we don't really know our furry friends until we've spent enough time with them.

Cats can be sweet and loveable, but they can also be rowdy and mischievous. By nature, these curious creatures like to know what's happening in their surroundings. They might follow us around as we go about our day, trying to assess what captures our attention. It turns out, they don't see us as their owners. They actually think of us as their equals—sometimes their lessers if we don't follow the rules—and they want to know what we're up to like we would our own human friends. Some cats may require extra attention, becoming disgruntled if we don't play or show them enough love.

Regardless of your cat's personality, felines aren't in the business of adapting to you and your routine. They will learn to pick up on your habits, schedules, and means of conduct, but they're not in the game of switching up who they are to accommodate *your* needs. You will need to learn to adapt to their ways, as this is the power of the cat. The sooner you learn how to make your cat happy, the better your life will be.

Body Language

Just like humans, cats tell us a lot about their mood through their body language. Understanding a cat takes time and dedication, but if you can master the art of "speaking cat," you will find your relationship with them to be much more rewarding. While this chart is meant to help you decipher your furry friend's mood at any given moment, please note that your cat can change their disposition without any warning. A cat's sense of mystery is the key to their power.

Here is a chart to help you better understand your cat:

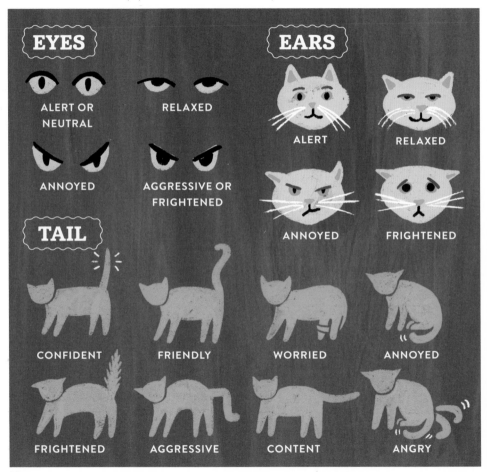

EYES

ALERT OR NEUTRAL

RELAXED

ANNOYED

AGGRESSIVE OR FRIGHTENED

EARS

ALERT

RELAXED

ANNOYED

FRIGHTENED

TAIL

CONFIDENT

FRIENDLY

WORRIED

ANNOYED

FRIGHTENED

AGGRESSIVE

CONTENT

ANGRY

BODY

CHILL

TRUSTING

FRIENDLY

PLAYFUL

ANNOYED

SCARED

HUNTING

WORRIED

WHISKERS

NEUTRAL

INTERESTED

FEARFUL

AGGRESSIVE

Meowing, Purring, and Other Odd Noises

Sometimes it's hard to tell whether your cat's meow is a greeting, or if they're trying to warn you that you're in mortal danger. The fun fact about meowing, as opposed to other cat sounds, is that these outbursts are geared specifically toward us humans! Kittens meow to their mothers to garner their attention, but as cats reach adolescence, they meow less frequently to their feline friends. Rather than a meow, adult cats resort to other sounds altogether when vocalizing issues with other members of their species.

A cat's meow can come in many different forms. Long, drawn-out meowing signals that your cat wants something from you such as food, access to a room, or to be let outside. A short, quick meow, or multiple mews, are often used as a cheerful greeting. Low-pitched meows indicate a complaint—most notably heard when their food bowl is empty. And a high-pitched meow usually signifies when your cat is startled or in pain, such as having their tail accidentally stepped on.

Here is a list of other sounds that cats make to express themselves:

CHIRP/CHATTER: *high-pitched bursts of sound, sometimes quick clicking noises.*	Cats make this sound when they are watching prey, such as birds, squirrels, or chipmunks, usually from behind a window where they cannot reach.
GROWL: *a low, grumbling sound.*	Cats growl out of fear, pain, or for territorial reasons.
HISS: *a quick burst of air as your cat exhales, similar to a snake.*	Cats hiss when they feel threatened. When a cat hisses, they keep their teeth exposed and their mouth wide open.
PURR: *a low, continuous fluttering sound.*	Cats purr when they feel the most happy and content. A cat may also purr to help soothe themselves if they are injured or sick.
TRILL: *a high-pitched muffled sound.*	This sound indicates that a cat is happy to greet you or a fellow cat. Mother cats trill as a way to get their kittens' attention.
YOWL: *a long, drawn-out moan.*	Cats yowl when they want to mate, are concerned about their territory, are in pain, or after they've captured their prey.

My Cat Hates Me

Cats are magical creatures. And while the universe sent us these little fluffers to warm our hearts, there are certainly times when we question if our cats really like us. Why do they keep shredding every roll of toilet paper we put out? Why do they sleep all day, only to keep us awake all night? And why do they freak out when we go to the bathroom without them?

Our precious felines do adore us, even though they may not show it at times (or most of the time). They appreciate the food we provide and the extra doses of catnip. They love our cuddles when some touchy time is needed, and the distance when silence is preferred. They treasure their warm shelter that provides peace and happy sleeps. But some say cats don't recognize that it's us humans who have actually provided this sanctuary. Rather, a cat believes we have migrated to this shared Pride Land of cozy blankets and food-on-demand together. Remember, equals!

If your cat seems angry or wants to hide under the bed, it's best to give your furry friend space. As equals, you wouldn't be too pleased if your roommate bothered you when you were in a bad mood, right? Cats may have pent up energy from not getting enough play time (hint: go drag a ribbon around the house for your cat to chase to help break up the monotony), or maybe they're not feeling the greatest, or have some aches and pains. Maybe your fur ball needs space from all the extra pettin' and lovin'. Sometimes, too much of a good thing is just too much. Or, maybe your cat is just not the social type. Not all breeds are Chatty Cathy's.

It's easy to believe your cat's mission in life is to mess with you, yet science tells us this isn't true—felines just have quirky behaviors. Try explaining why your cat will seek out water anywhere that isn't the water bowl next to the food. While we may never fully understand a cat's wishes and why they prefer shipping boxes for beds over the expensive cat bed we just bought, we love our cats unconditionally. As we pay closer attention to their personalities, their tail flicks, their sounds, and their opinions, we'll better understand how to make them happy. And the sooner we learn to respond to our cat's peculiar needs and behaviors, the sooner we ease any tension in the home, or more aptly, their kingdom.

PETTING METHODS THAT YOUR CAT (USUALLY) PREFERS

The Royal Crown Pet

WHERE TO PERFORM THIS PET:

NOSE TO HEAD

Place four fingers on the crown of your cat's head. Confidently place your thumb on the tip of their nose. Slowly slide your thumb up along the bridge of their nose, keeping all other fingers securely pressed to their head at all times. Repeat, if necessary. If your cat approves of the petting, try broadening your stroke to reach the temples between the eye and the ear. The temporal glands produce pheromones that cats use to mark their territory. Cats enjoy this pet because it helps them spread their oils onto you, claiming you as part of their territory, which you are.

You Can't Always Get What You Want Pet

**WHERE TO
PERFORM THIS PET:**

ARMPIT

We are all guilty of it. We walk into the room, catch our cat sleeping with curled paws dangling over a fluffy belly. We drop everything to run over and feverishly pet their tummy. Our love overwhelms our cat and they dart off, never to be seen again. Next time, control your enthusiasm and walk slowly over to your feline. Act like you have something else to do that is very important, like moving things around on your bookshelf a fraction of an inch. Once your cat is fooled, squat down and gently place your hand on their armpit. Massage in a slow circular motion, bypassing the belly altogether. Repeat on the other side, if possible. Opting to pet the second-rate armpits over the cute belly accomplishes two things: (1) your excitement level drops dramatically, thus showing constraint, and (2) your cat picks up on this remarkable feat, and rewards you by only waking you up twice that night.

You Had Me at Hello Pet

**WHERE TO
PERFORM THIS PET:**

UNDER THE CHIN

Another tried and true method of cat-petting is a gentle scratch under the chin. While not all cats like to be touched, or even looked at, a scratch under the hard-to-reach chin is one of the most accepted forms of petting a cat. Cats have a scent gland under the chin known as the submandibular. They use this gland to rub their oils onto their surroundings to mark their territory, including you. Begin the pet with your cat facing you. Palm side up, place your hand under the chin and run your fingers from the back of the jaw toward the front of the chin. Feel free to scratch as hard as your cat will allow, but mind your strength.

Five-Second Pet

With most petting methods, you must first determine if your cat is in the mood. Unlike attention-mongering dogs, a cat doesn't need you as much, so the Five-Second pet is the best way to find out if your cat will allow some affection. It's a quick acknowledgment that you and your feline coexist in each other's space, and they're able to get their pheromones all over you and claim you as theirs without taking too much time out of their day. Go for the scent glands in the cheeks, under the chin, behind the ears, or base of the tail. But make it quick! Your goal here is to play hard-to-get. Act indifferent and your cat might find you more interesting.

May the Force Be with You Pet

Cats' cheeks are prime real estate for petting. Whether you choose to pet your feline's choppers or not, they will seek out areas around your home, or outside, against which to rub their furry faces. This is called "bunting," and allows for a cat to mark their territory by transferring oils, or pheromones, onto nearby objects. Using one or two hands, stroke your cat's cheekbones behind the whisker line. Depending on your cat's mood, they may prefer a more rigorous pet. Clench your fists and massage more intensely using your knuckles. Don't be surprised if this pet only lasts fifteen seconds or less. Again, it's all about the oil transfer with cats and once you have served them, they are done.

Distract-a-Pet

Belly rubs, as we have already discussed, are tricky. Some cats like their torso rubbed, while others prefer you keep your paws to yourself. It's a good rule of thumb to always approach the abdomen with caution when trying to pet a cat. If a cat lies on their back with belly exposed, assume they trust their environment. However, they may prefer you simply look and not touch. A cat's underside is a vulnerable place and most cats don't like the spare tire rubbed. If you find your cat lying on their back, try placing your hand gently under their armpit. This point of contact may distract your cat while you slowly inch your way toward the belly. An alternative to the armpit hold would be to either gently secure the cat's leg, tail, or ear with your hand. It's crucial to note that this pet is only made possible by the fact that you are distracting your feline with one hand, while the other sneaks in a cute belly rub. Without the distraction, attempts may be futile.

To Belly, or Not to Belly Pet

**WHERE TO
PERFORM THIS PET:**

BELLY

This position requires you to sit on the floor, or any flat surface, with legs straight out and knees touching. If your cat will allow it, gently encourage them to lie on their back between your legs. A light scratch under the chin is almost always welcome and may help coax your cat into assuming this position. Beginning in a counterclockwise motion, massage your cat's belly in large circular motions to encompass the entire width of the torso. Your cat may prefer clockwise, so feel free to try again in the opposite direction if your cat hasn't already left you. Once you've determined which direction your cat likes the most, move your way down the belly, but not past the legs. Don't stay in any one area too long, as your cat will sense your control of the situation. Once that happens, the pet is surely over.

I Put a Spell on You Pet

**WHERE TO
PERFORM THIS PET:**

BETWEEN AND
BEHIND THE EARS

A little scratch to the top of the head is usually welcome as this is an area that your cat can't reach. Feel free to scratch with your fingernails between and behind the ears, adding pressure to your cat's liking. They may tilt their head and lean in to you as they cherish your loving touch (or they may walk away—note: good to test out the five-second pet here to see if the cold shoulder is imminent). With oil from the pinna glands at the base of the ear, this is another way that your cat likes to transfer pheromones onto you. If it bothers you that your cat has these ulterior motives, feel free to mix it up. Stop the rub and look the other way. The added sense of mystery will keep them wondering who owns who.

All the Good Feels Pet

Most cats enjoy their whole back rubbed from head to tail. Start this pet at the base of the neck and run your hand continuously down the spine to the tail. Keep your hand on your cat throughout the entire pet. If you're too slow, your cat will get annoyed. If you're too fast, your cat will get annoyed. Find the right speed that works best for your fuzzy friend. Don't worry if your cat darts off when you try to perform the All The Good Feels. You can always play their game and run away when they rub up against your leg, and see how they like it.

No Sun = No Fun Pet

WHERE TO PERFORM THIS PET:

UPPER CHEST TO NECK

Cats expend a lot of energy during the day chasing imaginary flying squirrels around the house. When the sun shines through the windows, your cat's internal battery knows to recharge its energy reserves. Give your furry friend a moment to rest in the sun. The solar power helps your cat conserve calories to regulate their body temperature.
If you absolutely must pet your sleepy kitty, a light scratch to the upper chest and neck is acceptable (note: if your cat is in bread-loaf position, this pet will not work). Start by placing your hand on your cat's chest and lightly stroke up and down. Slide up to the neck and scratch with your fingertips, trying not to disrupt your cat's sunbathing session. If you wake your cat, they may seek revenge by waking you in the middle of the night to bring you presents you didn't request.

The Universe Is on Your Side Pet

Not everyone is lucky and ends up with a sweet, cuddly cat. If you got stuck with a crabby feline, or one that bunkers down in the bowels of your basement all day, petting opportunities are slim. However, if you get a chance, one of the surest ways to win their heart is a soft caress to the ears. Softly place your hand on top of your cat's head. Cup the cat's ear between your thumb and forefinger and run your hand in a circular motion. It's okay to flap their ear as you roll in all directions. This full ear massage releases the golden nuggets, or subglandular scent oils, onto your hands, marking you as your cat's safe zone. Each time your scaredy cat anoints you with their oils, you are one step closer to enlightenment.

The Booty Lift Pet

Most cats enjoy being pet on the lower back right above the tail. Some cats prefer a gentle touch, while others enjoy a firmer, rougher pet. You might even notice your cat raising their back in an arching motion, or they may begin to lick and purr. Start this pet on the lower back and swiftly move your hand toward the base of the tail. Feel free to add more pressure as you work your way down. Some cats don't mind a grasp to the tail base with a slight shake from side to side, or even a soft pat.

I Need That Catnip on My Desk Yesterday Pet

WHERE TO PERFORM THIS PET:

BACK OF NECK

Does your cat jump up on you while you're trying to work? Do they prance around your desk, weaving in and out of your computer cords and coffee while they swat your pens onto the floor? Once your cat jitterbugs across the keyboard looking to plop down, you can choose to shoo them away, or cave in and caress them as a little gift for wanting to be near you. Assuming your cat wins and is planted firmly on your keyboard, reward them with a back of the neck massage. Run your fingers from below the neck up to the top of the head. Your cat might find this massage very relaxing and lower their head to absorb all the feels. You've probably just earned yourself another night free from a violent puking session on your favorite rug.

You're Wasting Your Time Pet

WHERE TO PERFORM THIS PET:

ON THE SIDE

Side rubs are neither here nor there for your cat. It's basically a waste of a rub. This pet is great if you aren't feeling confrontational—you can selfishly sneak in a pet while not annoying your cat in the slightest. Don't underestimate the power of the cat and their ability to annoy you back. Ever wonder why they prefer to use your leather chair as their favorite scratching post? To perform the You're Wasting Your Time, wait for your cat to recline on their side. With a gentle touch to the back of the head, work your way down their side toward the tail, aiming closer to the spine. Avoid touching the legs or belly area as your cat will do one, or all, of three things: (1) clench your forearm with their front claws holding you hostage, (2) lockjaw their teeth into your arm, or (3) thwack you with their back-kicky legs like an angry kangaroo.

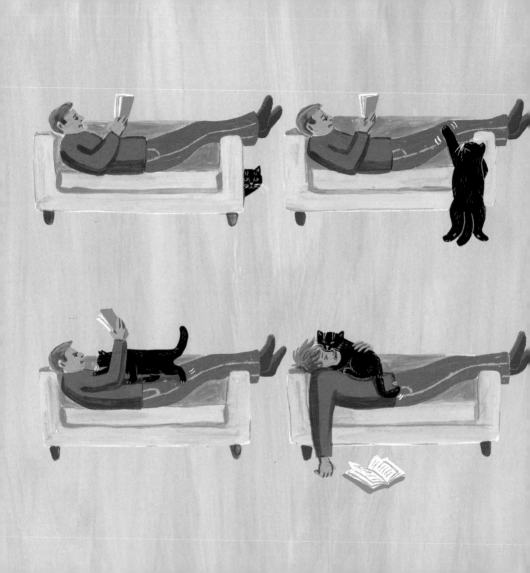

I Don't Make the Rules Except for When I Do Pet

Surprisingly, or not so surprisingly, if you know this from experience, some cats are a little needier than others. Perhaps they've hung around with some of their canine counterparts and adopted the belief that personal space is unnecessary. We're not talking about the cat who follows you around the house whenever you exit the room. We're talking about the furry friend who jumps up on your lap or chest and demands you stay put for an indefinite amount of time—could be all night or could just be for two seconds if only to remind you that they are superior. At this point, any light touch down the back, around the ears, or under the chin is most welcome. If your cat is being extra needy, it's possible that they may have separation anxiety or attachment issues. It's also entirely possible that they may simply want to assert their dominance over you. You may be forced to give up other activities so you can stay home and pet your cat more. Sorry, I don't make the rules, and neither do you.

PETTING METHODS THAT ANNOY YOUR CAT

The Overstimulated Pet

WHERE TO
PERFORM THIS PET:

ANYWHERE

While most cats like to be petted from time to time, too much of a good thing can put anyone over the edge. Take cues from your feline. If they seem to enjoy your caresses at first, feel free to continue petting your cat. If your cat starts to twitch their tail or take a light nip at you, this is a sign that they need to rest and would prefer not to be touched at this time. Try again later.

That Awkward Moment Pet

Just because you like holding hands doesn't
mean your cat does, too. A gentle touch to the
paw can easily cost you a few points. Be prepared
for rejection, dirty looks, or a firm claw-hold
to your forearm. Blame it on the mood, the day, or
the weather, but to your cat's defense, there are
scientific reasons that explain why many cats aren't
paw holders. Felines have a web of nerve receptors
in their paws that warn them of temperature,
texture, pressure, and even vibration changes within
their environment. These highly sensitive pads are
a cat's main line of defense. While some of us can't
handle the paw rub rejection, it is best to not waste
your time. Find something else to do.

This Is Not a Hair Salon Pet

WHERE TO PERFORM THIS PET:

FROM TAIL TO HEAD

There are just some things in life that are simply not right. Trying to give your cat a mini-Mohawk is one of them. Their hair is meant to be sleek and go in one direction only. Your cat prefers to keep their hair in place to help regulate body temperature. By petting your cat's fur backwards, you create tufts of hair that stick up, allowing heat to escape. Cats have a higher body temperature than humans, so they need the fur to keep their bodies warm. Besides trying to remedy the annoying feeling of hair follicles going against the grain, cats will lick their coat back into place to remove unwanted scents from their body. Your "unwanted scent" cuts into your cat's napping time as they have to groom themselves in hard to reach places. Annoying.

Don't Think I Don't Know What You've Done Pet

WHERE TO PERFORM THIS PET:

LEG

A cat's legs are like chicken wings—there's not much meat on the bone. If you like touching these bony extremities, try petting when your cat has one or two stretchy paws out front. Cats aren't into leg-petting because they're afraid you're going to get some crazy ideas and it will lead to touching their sensitive paws. If you're so determined to caress your cat's furry legs, try petting them when your feline is distracted. Feel free to use catnip or treats for maximum distraction. But remember, a cat never truly gets distracted. They know full well what's going on around them. You've crossed the line and a door scratching session will be coming soon. Tough luck.

Don't Wake the Bear Pet

Don't forget the reason you got a cat. You liked the idea of your furry friend not jumping up on you and slobbering all over your face the second you walk into a room. Show your cat some respect and return the favor. If your cat is sleeping when you enter the room, don't go nutso and suffocate them with your love. Your cat won't forget your crazy impulses and will wake you in the middle of the night to (a) bite your toes, (b) knock stuff off of your nightstand, (c) meow loudly for no good reason, or (d) violently heave hairballs on your shag carpet.

Can't Let Go Pet

No one is proud to admit they've performed the Can't Let Go, but we've all done it. The Can't Let Go is when you want to pet your cat and your cat wants nothing to do with you. Basically, you've got so much love to give and you want your cuddly fluffball to have it all. You start petting your cat as they try to walk away. Thinking you can win them over with your love, you pet their back harder and harder. Your cat succumbs to the pressure and drops to the floor, shimmying their way out of your grasp. Since you missed the memo about "if you love something, set it free," this is an opportunity to finally learn your lesson, accept the rejection, and move on. Try channeling your energy into something positive, like writing a book about how to pet your cat.

Sending Out an S.O.S. Pet

WHERE TO PERFORM THIS PET:

TAIL

A cat sends out secret signals to the world using their tail. As humans, we don't always pick up on what they're broadcasting, but other cats get the message loud and clear. A low-hanging rigid tail might mean danger, while an upright tail with a hook at the end means good times ahead. Cats' tails also provide balance and stability as they walk and jump up on your refrigerator. These furry extremities are very sensitive—they're full of nerves, tiny blood vessels, vertebrae, and ligaments. It's no wonder your cat may not like a tail rub of any kind. You're messing with their control tower and they may launch a counter strike.

You've Got That Lov'n Feelin' Pet

WHERE TO PERFORM THIS PET:

BELLY

Do you clench your teeth when you pet your cat's fuzzy tummy? Has your lovin' feelin' overwhelmed you as you pet with more vigor? Your love may be your cat's worst nightmare as your petting grows faster and more intense. Cats' bellies are vulnerable places, home to many of their vital organs. Give your fur ball a break and step back. Your cat is trying to stage their quickest and most direct escape route. Don't be surprised if your cat starts learning how to work the locks.

I Haven't Sniffed You Yet Pet

HEAD

When you pet a cat, especially for the first time, let them take a whiff of your hand first. Cats want to know if you pass the sniff test. If they don't like you and you continue to pet them, the clock starts ticking. They've got to work overtime to clean your oils off their head because they don't want your stink. Head-cleanings take time—where are they going to find that time, between all the naps they have to take? No way. It may seem a bit over the top that your cat has to sanitize their head every time you've touched them, but it does make you wonder what they really think about you.

Don't Trigger the Alarm System Pet

**WHERE TO
PERFORM THIS PET:**

WHISKERS

Your cat's whiskers are like magical sensors. While they don't have any feeling in the hair strands themselves, the movement to the hair follicle warns of objects getting too close to their face or eyes. Whiskers also sense the critical movement of animals being hunted or prey in the area. If you're obsessed with petting your cat's whiskers, try a little rub to the follicle area by the cheek. This will give your cat the added benefit of spreading territorial pheromones onto you. Avoid touching the hair strands or tips of the whiskers, as this will probably annoy your cat. Have you ever found a crusty hairball caked in the carpet behind the sofa? Cats have no problem seeking revenge by leaving hidden treasures.

I'm Not Your Baby Pet

WHERE TO PERFORM THIS PET:

BETWEEN THE PAW PADS

It's so easy to forget that our cats are not mini humans. Sometimes we want to hold and rock them like little babies, or plop them down on our laps for a big hug, or even worse, play dress-up. And sometimes, just like babies, our cats get their paws into trouble. Most cats don't like having their paws rubbed, so the I'm Not Your Baby pet is the way to go if you need to check for any problems with their claws or pads. Gently set your cat on your lap, belly side up. With front paws resting in your hands, feed them a treat, or two, or three. Cats are above your tricks, unless your tricks involve treats. Try caressing your cat's paws between the pads where there are more scent glands. If everything looks okay, it's best to end the pet now. Eventually your cat will remind you that they are of the superior feline family, and not your play baby, so it's better to quit while you're ahead.

Resources

Cat Behavior Associates: http://www.catbehaviorassociates.com.
Pam Johnson-Bennett is a cat behavior expert and has starred on the Animal Planet UK series *Psycho Kitty*. She has written eight books on cat behavior.

The Spruce Pets: http://www.thesprucepets.com.
A Veterinary Review Board comprised of top board-certified vet professionals. Article referenced: "Why Cats Groom Themselves So Often," by Amy Shojai, certified animal behavior consultant and author of twenty-seven pet care books: https://www.thesprucepets.com/why-cats-groom-themselves-so-often-4126526.

Jackson Galaxy: http://www.jacksongalaxy.com.
Host of the Animal Planet series *My Cat from Hell*. YouTube video referenced: "Why Scent Marking Matters: The Ultimate Cat Confidence": https://www.youtube.com/watch?time_continue=1&v=vzljCggDL-Y&feature=emb_logo.

Purina: http://www.purina.co.uk.
The leader in nutrition and health research in the pet industry. Article referenced, "What Do Different Cat Noises Mean?": https://www.purina.co.uk/cats/behaviour-and-training/understanding-cat-behaviour/what-do-cat-sounds-mean.

The Cat Coach: http://www.thecatcoach.com.
Marilyn Krieger is an internationally recognized cat behavior specialist and award-winning author.

ASPCA: http://www.aspca.org.
American Society for the Prevention of Cruelty to Animals. Article referenced: "Meowing and Yowling," https://www.aspca.org/pet-care/cat-care/common-cat-behavior-issues/meowing-and-yowling.

Some Special Cats

While all cats are beyond special, here are a few that I had the pleasure of painting for this book:

Rocco – "the perpetually embarrassed"
Theo – "the overly confident"
Cat Parent: Me (@angelastaehling)

Tsunami (@tsunabulous) – "the always hungry"
Monsoon (@mesmerizingmonsoon) – "the ultimate clingy baby"
Storm (@stormsuperstar) – "the sassy diva"
Cat Parent: Cyril Sontillano (@cyrilcybernated)

Olive – "the unexpectedly fierce"
Willow – "the adorably shy"
Cat Parent: Lauren Wong (@everyday_olive)

Penny – "the annoyed"
Cat Parent: Karl Stevens (@karlstevensart)

Floyd – "the lover"
Cat Parents: Susie Floros & Cami Garrison (@FloydTheLion)

BenBen (@benbencatcat) - "the cheese eater"
Cat Parents: Sandy (@benbencatmom) and Adam (@benbencatdad)

Scout – "the very loud about it"
Cat Parent: my book editor, Olivia Roberts

Andy – "the audacious"
Cat Parent: my brother, Mike Barbaro

Milo – "the dreamer"
Moose – "the ruffian"
Cat Parent: my sister, Chief Barbaro